Break the Line
Analysis & Method in Attacking Rugby

Rick L. Ferrara

Note to Readers:

Learn rugby with a coach. Play safe. The author has worked diligently to make sure the concepts herein are technically accurate. However, neither the author nor the publisher can accept responsibility for any injury or loss sustained a result of the use of this material.

Rights:

All rights reserved. No part of this publication may be reproduced, stored in a retrieval system, or transmitted in any form or by any means, electronic, mechanical, photocopying, recording or otherwise, without the prior written permission of the Author and Publisher.

ISBN Information:

ISBN-13: 978-1542325790 / ISBN-10: 154232579X

Copyright Notice

All content within this book, including the words and diagrams, is authored by and with exclusive copyright to Rick L. Ferrara of Cleveland, Ohio, USA, 2017 ©

Cover photo is courtesy of t-fizzle photography, Cleveland, Ohio at Tfizzlephotography.com, and featuring Kevin McLaughlin of the Cleveland Rovers and Taryn Avon of the Cleveland Crusaders

Published by Rick L. Ferrara, 2077 E. 4th Street, 2nd Floor, Cleveland, Ohio, 44115 and via Amazon.com and Createspace.com. Follow Rick on Twitter: @RL_Ferrara

Acknowledgments & Thanks

My rugby career started the night I watched a video of my friend Jeff playing rugby at Ashland University. When my next college semester started, I attended the next club practice and never looked back.

Thank you to my rugby brethren, starting with my first coach at Marquette University, Boris Turcinovic, to whom I owe a great deal, my first backline coach Yan, and teammates from Marquette University, especially my lifelong friends Alejandro, Paddy, and England. Thanks go to Chin and Big Wally for providing my first coaching experience and being such good men, and to all the Homestead Highlanders and their families for their support, commitment, and friendship.

Thanks to all my Cleveland Rovers teammates, especially Craig for the intro to the team and his brotherhood, and Dale, Paul, Dave, and Sean for the leadership and guidance. Thanks goes to Matt and Jason for giving me my first coaching opportunity in Cleveland, and to Brian, Tom, Ryan, Trip, Nails, Mike, Nemeth, Sean, Buddy, Doc Widow, John, and Bryan for sharing some or all of an incredible five year stretch in my rugby life. And thank you to all my St. Edward Eagle brothers that allowed me to work with them on their games. And of course, to my wife Courtney, for attending all the matches and events, interrupting her own life, watching me write at the kitchen table, and being a part of something I feel is special.

Many thanks for the support of the Cleveland Rovers and Cleveland Crusaders as this book has been launched, especially Ryan, Jason, Dale, Danny, Will, Mark, Dimes, Taryn & Kevin.

Outside of the rugby world, I owe much to authors like GM Lev Albert, GM Roman Dzindzichashvili, and GM Eugen Perelshteyn, of *Chess Openings for White/Black, Explained* and my study thereof for the tone and approach of this book.

Table of Contents

- ❖ Introduction   *p. 5*
  - Purpose of the Book
  - Description of the Diagrams

- ❖ <u>Ch. 1: Elements of Attack</u>   *p. 13*
  - Initiative
  - Ball Speed
  - Off-the-Ball Movement
  - Communication

- ❖ <u>Ch. 2: Tactics Using the Elements of Attack</u>   *p. 21*
  - *Section 1:* Exploiting Numerical Advantages   *p. 23*
    - The Pin
    - The Scissor – Two Versus One
  - *Section 2:* Attacking Defects in the Defense   *p.37*
    - The Bounce – Against Misaligned Defenses of Equal Number
    - The Crash – Against Wide and Staggered Defenses of Equal Number
    - The Dummy Scissor – Against Staggered Defenses of Equal Number
    - The Loop – Against Wide and Staggered Defenses of Equal Number
  - *Section 3:* Combo Tactics That Create Defects in the Defense   *p. 55*
    - The Scissor Pin – For Numerical Advantages with Tight Spacing
    - The Scissor Crash – Against Even Numbers and a Flat Defense

- ❖ <u>Ch. 3 : Application of the Elements and Tactics to Structured Play</u>   *p. 67*
  - Reading the Defense – Analytically Breaking Down a Defense
  - Example – Applying Analytics to a Sample Situation
  - Attack Key – A Primer for Applying the Correct Tactics
  - Adjustments – A Note on Flat Backlines

- ❖ Conclusion   *p. 89*

Break the Line – Analysis & Method 4

Introduction

This book is written for rugby players and coaches of all levels who want to learn more about the open-field ground attack in rugby union.

And I mean that exclusively - this book is only meant to focus on attacking in space and while keeping the ball in-hand. It does not discuss kicking attacks, kicking tactics, or close-quarters play in the forwards. By focusing so narrowly on a part of the game of rugby, I hope to provide a more in-depth examination of how that part functions. This approach also presents a more manageable book to the reader. There are certainly enough concepts within the open-field ground attack for this type of treatment.

This book does refer to "backline" play, but it is not meant to be exclusively applied to backline players. Forwards learning these ideas will be better off than those that do not, especially in a system that allows them to float into the backline or where the backline is made indistinguishable.

The diagramming and discussion in this book is meant to approach the study of parts of the game of rugby like one would approach the study of the game of chess. Since some of the interactions in rugby can be viewed as a perfect, or near-perfect information game, and a near-sequential movement game for the offense, they can be studied as such. The language in the book speaks to *ideal* approaches, sharp movements, initiative, forcing, and tempo much like a book on chess, even if rugby is played under more abstract circumstances.

The diagrams are information rich, and should be intuitive. Painstaking attention has been dedicated to the spacing, lining, and descriptions in the forty-odd diagrams in the book. It is all intentional. The diagrams include what a rugby diagram should include – when to sprint, what space to attack, and what space to avoid. They are also notable because they provide a look only at the most important moment of an attack; at the point of a critical decision.

That being said, the book can be read from beginning to end, or can be explored by jumping between concepts. It will ultimately best serve the reader as reference for offensive reflection, diagnosis, and playmaking.

With these characteristics, I do believe this book presents an analytical approach that is unique. These ideas have been developed and applied in all of the clubs I coached, and within each game I played. They worked for me and my players, and so that is why I share them with you.

The Tackle Line – *Breaking the Tackle Line prior to the Gain Line*

The object of this entire book is to focus players on breaking an imaginary line on the field: the "tackle" line. The tackle line is prior to the "gain" line, where the defense has positioned its players in an attempt to stop an offense. This book will start with the simplest advantages that allow a team to break the tackle line, and then analyze the more complex advantages that accomplish the same.

Gain Line: Lateral line across the pitch, bisecting the ball, where the last breakdown or set piece occurred.

Tackle Line: Line where the defense (triangles) physically encounters the offensive attack (circles), which is approximated here from a scrum:

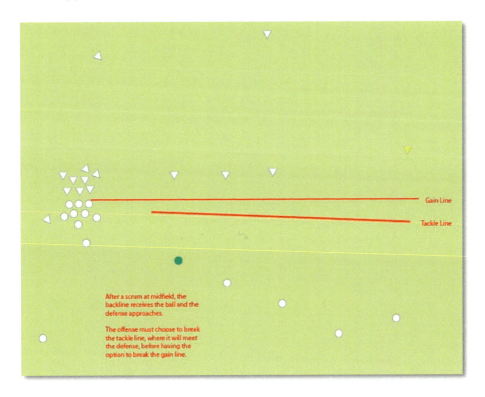

After a scrum at midfield, the backline receives the ball and the defense approaches.

The offense must choose to break the tackle line, where it will meet the defense, before having the option to break the gain line.

Without a focus on breaking the tackle line, an offensive backline makes a critical error. That same backline will typically run its attack to the gain line instead, and the tactics employed will not develop fast enough to be effective. The focus of every attack in rugby must necessarily be where the defense *will be* once the play develops. The focus cannot be where the defense *was*.

This type of anticipation allows the attackers to time their attack properly and have a realistic expectation of which tactics will work, and which will not. Thus, it is imperative for the backline to focus on first breaking the tackle line. They will breach the gain line in due time.

The Diagrams – *Improving on the Status Quo*

Existing rugby diagrams, available online and in the manuals preceding this one, are not detailed enough. I decided to rethink the rugby diagram to convey the principles that are promoted in this book, and hopefully provide a fresh look at attacking rugby.

Here is an example, miniaturized for this section only, which previews the detail that will be provided in the diagrams I've produced for this book.

Offensive players are circles, with the green circle being the ball carrier.

Defensive players are triangles.

The lines are where the runner has already ran.

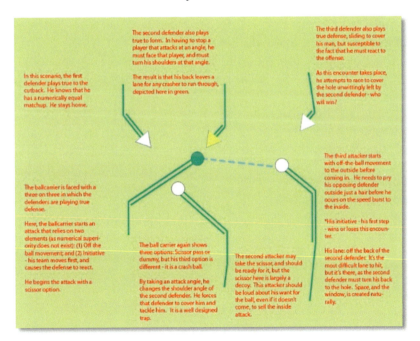

Features of the Basic Diagrams

Multiple Speeds (Single Line / Double Line):
The single line in the diagram shows a standard speed and direction, running at 80-90%, while a double line shows 100% speed, known commonly as a "burst", taken typically at or around the tackle line, or to catch up with an attack at the tackle line.

Sharp Angles to Show Abrupt Changes in Direction:
The angles are meant to be sharp, for reasons of offensive advantage, and typically the diagrams will show offensive players making off the ball movement of some kind. Take special care to note the angles of attack before the tackle line is met and before the offensive players hit their speed burst.

Defender Movement and Shoulder Angles:
Each defender's speed and angle will be shown, as if an arrow. Their shoulder angle, diagrammed as the bottom of the triangle, is also shown. The "bottom" or flat part of the triangle is the back of the defender, while the point is his nose.

Passing Lines (Blue Dotted Lines):
The blue dotted line can be either a potential or actual pass made during a given situation, to show either the option to pass or how the ball carrier received the ball. Finding the ball carrier, in green, shows you how he received the ball and how he might use it.

Focus of Attack (Yellow Defender):
The yellow defender is the "target" of the attack. It is his defensive movement that is the most important, as one player is typically made the focus of the attack, be it a pin or a crash.

Features of the Enhanced Diagrams

This book also provides a new form of enhanced diagram that will provide additional information on the technique involved. Here is a sample, miniaturized, that shows some of the depth in the diagrams, with the following features:

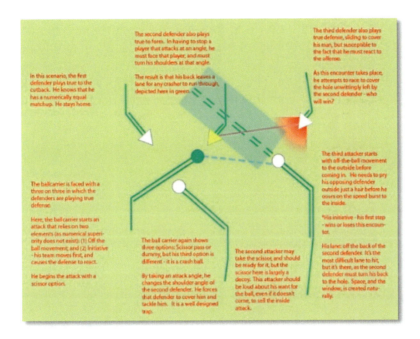

Defender Strengths (Red Rays):
Red emanating from a defender shows an area of tackling strength, while the absence of red shows the tackler's weakness.

Windows (Purple Line Between Key Defenders):
Windows, depicted in purple, show the ideal plane through which a player should break the tackle line. You'll see why those windows are typically at an angle, not a flat line across the field.

Crashing Lanes (Green Rectangle):
A green rectangle shows a safe crashing lane past the crashing window and *behind* a defender, a typical weakness in a defense, with the *potential* crashing line through that rectangle, shown as a dotted line.

Time-Lapse Play Breakdowns:
Where a play is complex, we will take our time looking at each step of the attack. Typically only one pass is shown (in light blue), and the action after the pass is not. This is because, if the diagrams are clear, the possibilities are obvious. Notes will clarify any ambiguities.

Notes:
The diagrams tell a better story with the notes. Each note is close to its subject attacker or defender.

Chapter 1
Elements of Attack

The elements of attacking are the very basic principles that always apply to the offense in rugby. You should be able to share them with your teammates and students repeatedly, because they are indisputable truths.

These elements are the *advantages* the attacking players have, which are distinct from the *actions* players should take, which are covered in Chapter 2.

It is commonly known that players should attack space, use support players around them in an attack, and be active in supporting the ball carrier. Those players should also strive to score, which is the privilege of possession. Those directives, however, still beg questions about the manner of or reason for doing so. Only by exploring the questions behind those directives can an offense hone its effectiveness.

The advantages are identifiable as initiative, ball speed, off-the-ball movement, and communication. We will explore them in depth here.

Elements of Advantage

1. Initiative – *The Option to Direct Action*
The prime advantage of the offense is that it carries the ball and has the option to change the direction and speed of play, all without telling the defense. It is the option to *act first*, and thus force the defense to settle for *reacting*. The offense can exaggerate their advantage with drastic changes in the direction and speed of play.

- **Varying Speed**

One component of the offense's advantage is the ability to vary the speed of an attack. When this concept is applied to the ball carrier, it suggests that the ball carrier can gain an offensive advantage by altering his speed when he carries the ball. This is because running at a constant speed is more predictable, and thus defendable. Altering one's speed is a *change* that is less predictable.

Thus, an offensive player has much to gain from applying speed at the proper moment in time and space. This hidden "burst" of speed is meant to be applied before the defense can react in time to defend the change.

- **Varying Direction**

The other component of initiative is the ability of the offense to vary the direction of an attack at will. Applied to the ball carrier, it suggests an approach to the defender that maximizes the ball carrier's option to gain field position while limiting the defender's option to tackle.

An offensive player should endeavor to change direction towards open space, and force the defender to his side or back, to make a tackle more difficult and breaking the tackle line more likely. Changing direction quickly, and the angle of attack sharply exaggerates this advantage to the defender's detriment.

A ball carrier demonstrates a successful change of speed and direction by achieving "lane separation," a term that will be relied on throughout this book. Lane separation is when any offensive player, with or without the ball, evades a defending player by leaving a tackle lane.

The tackle lane is the prime tackling space forward of a defender. The ball carrier must apply initiative to leave that space, or lane – typically an extreme change in both speed and direction:

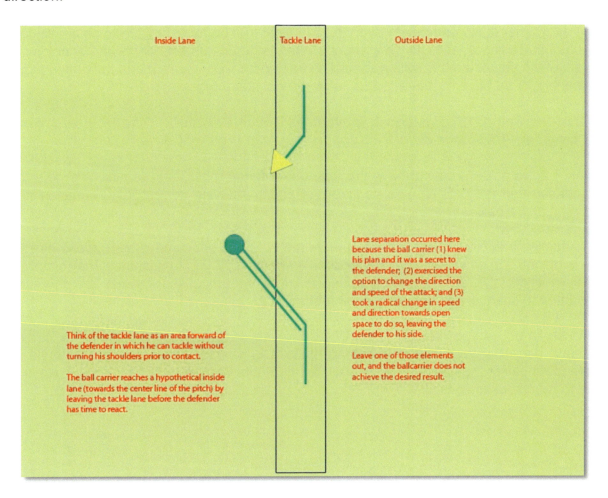

2. **Ball Speed Exceeds Running Speed -** *The Reason for Having Support that is Spaced and Available*

The ball, whether kicked or passed, travels faster than a defender can travel the same distance. An attacking team can utilize that to their advantage in numerous ways, by spacing themselves properly to allow the speed of the ball, when passed to create gains in field position.

The ball carrier thus need not do everything himself, but he must be able to pass accurately at a moment's notice, exploiting the areas where the defenders cannot cover. By holding the object of the game, the ball, with a special characteristic that it can exceed the running speed of any player on the field, the attacker has a distinct advantage.

3. **Off-the-Ball (OTB) Position & Movement Draws Reaction –** *The How and Why of Exacting Advantage Before a Support Player is the Ball Carrier*

Even if an attacker does not have the ball, the defense must react to him. He gets to do something that the defense has no luxury of doing - moving deceptively in relation to the position of the ball.

An attacker in support of the ball carrier has the option to show movement in one direction, while planning to attack in another direction. A crashing player, for instance, may simply drift to an outside lane, all the while planning to run a pattern to the inside. The defender is obligated to shadow that non-ball carrying attacker.

This slight advantage creates potential for the attacking team to manipulate a defender through deceptive movements, either to make a gap wider or to change the angle of a defender against the offense. In the end, the defender can be forced to move in ways that are to his disadvantage.

4. Communication – *The Inherent Advantage of Creating an Imperfect Information Game for Your Opponent*

The offense has an advantage in communication. The simplest example is that a backline may call a play that is a secret to the defense. That called play is unknown to the defense.

This keeps the game one of near "perfect information" for the offense, like chess. At the same time, it make the game one of "imperfect information" for the defense, like poker.

In short, the offense can see the likely plan of the defense, but the defense is kept from learning the plan of the offense. This has obvious advantages when combined with initiative, because the defense is then made doubly unaware of how to react to the coordinated offensive attack. The defense is then less able to defend the offense.

But what of loose play, where no play is called?

The communications advantage still exists in open field play, given some pre-planning by the offense. For example, the attackers should all acknowledge a chain of command that starts with the ball carrier. Through the ball carrier's words, hand gestures, and movements, the offense can be directed in the attack. For example, as the ball carrier breaks at a thirty-five degree angle ten meters from the sideline, with a support player on the sideline, what is he communicating?

Most likely a "scissor" or "switch" attempt, which we will discuss fully later. If he makes the same movement in open space, that movement can be construed the same way, so long as the players are familiar with each other's body language and movements. A shout of "Scissor, scissor!" or shouting "Outside, outside!" will clarify discrepancies. Adding a pointing finger to where the ball carrier wants the support person to be will also help.

In the below diagram, explained later in the section on combination tactics, a break on an angle with a 3 on 2 offensive advantage communicates the attack to the support players instantly:

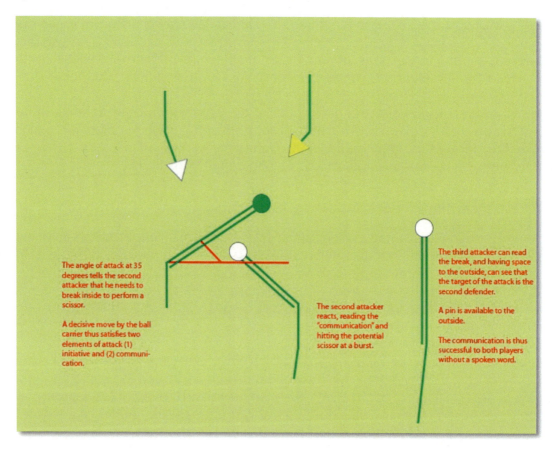

Even the ball carrier's straight approach to the tackle line can be construed as a "communication", if simply based on the realities that approaching a defense presents:

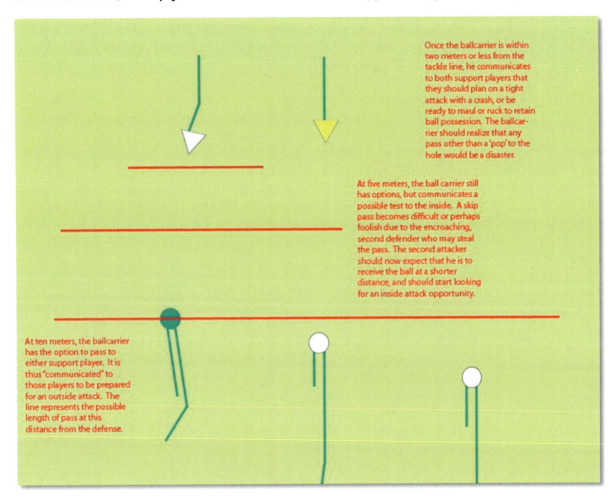

In rugby, this sort of communication takes on special importance because there little to no stoppage of play, and the ball carrier needs to coordinate his supporting cast in order to be successful. If he is able to act first and also communicate instantaneously to his support, he exacts a significant advantage over the defense, even if the offense and defense are equal in athletic ability, fitness, strength, and skill.

Applied together, these tactics become greater than the sum of their parts. They augment each other, make each other more powerful, and empower the players who use them.

When attacks fail, a player or coach can look back at the elements to analyze the source of the failure. Did the attackers sharply change angle and speed to space to create lane separation? Did the ball carrier pass the ball so slowly that the defender tracked in down? Were the attackers positioned so close together as to not take advantage of the field given to them? Did the support players not move off-the ball prior to the play, keeping their defensive counterpart in check? All of these are valid questions relating to the use of the elements of attack.

These questions become more relevant when viewed in light of each tactic in Chapter 2.

Chapter 2
Tactics Using the Elements of Attack

Each element can be applied to tactics, which then can become part of your strategy.

The focus of this chapter is on identifying and exploiting winnable situations. Once an advantage has been identified, the offense is expected to break the tackle line by exploiting that advantage. You as a coach or player should be thinking about your tactical advantages every time your team gains possession, at each set piece, and in each phase of play. In open field play, you should be able to identify the situation that reveals an advantage and act on it immediately.

But it starts here. An attacker first needs to be able to identify every tactical advantage.

That starts with the most common and best understood advantage, covered in section one, which is numbers. Literally, it is having a greater number of players in a given space than there are defenders. At its most basic, the advantage is two versus one. By exploring that simple advantage we can see how a numbers advantage can be exploited using the elements we know from Chapter 1. We can then draw some reliable conclusions about what it means to attack with three versus two, and four versus three.

The more nuanced advantage is covered in section two, whereby an offense encounters a defense that is misaligned, staggered, or wide. Even when the defense has equal numbers to the offense, it can be weak. These sorts of defects, in the way a defense approaches the tackle line, can be exploited by an observant offense given the proper tools.

And lastly, in section three we explore situations in which the offense creates advantage by applying combination tactics. Combination tactics can *create* defects in the defense, even when the defense is presenting equal numbers to the offense, or is playing the offense to its advantage. The offense, if mastering and applying all of the elements of attack, can make a losing situation into a winning situation, should it so choose.

The tactics that "win" those advantages are catalogued throughout this chapter, from the simplest to the most complex.

Chapter 2, Section 1
Capitalizing on Numerical Superiority

The most common tactical maneuver in the game is to attack with numerical superiority. Typically two persons versus one, three versus two, or four versus three, and so on.

This is often called an "overload", but that term leaves a lot to be desired. I don't use it a lot here without further description, because it is vague by itself and often times conjures the image of an outside advantage. A numerical superiority, on the other hand, provides an advantage to the outside or inside. The key characteristic is the difference in numbers in a defined space.

Having a numerical advantage is significant because, except in rare instances, a defender cannot move to physically cover the space occupied by two attackers. There is no time for the defender to do so, and the laws of physics demand that his body be in one place at any given time. This is embodied by the element from Chapter 1 – the ball moves faster than any defender.

Tactics based on numerical advantage should be the foundation of your open-field attacking philosophy. Such tactics pervade the entire game, and cannot be stressed enough. It seems rudimentary, but as you will see through the detail in this section, a backline can succeed merely by looking for numerical advantages - again, and again, and again.

The Pin – Against a Single Defender Pitted in the Lane Between Two Attackers

Pinning is the attacker's answer to the most pure numerical advantage - two versus one. It occurs when one defender plays in a lane between two attackers, attempting to force an error by the ball carrier.

The attacking team maintains a distinct advantage on each pin. The ball carrier should force the defender to commit by taking a hard line to the inside, giving the ball carrier the opportunity to pass to the available support player, who then breaks the tackle line:

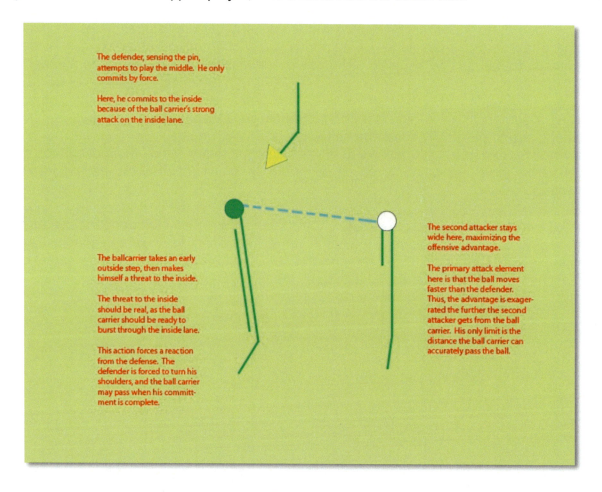

Break the Line – Analysis & Method

Note that angles represent how and when a cut is made, and when a speed burst is applied by both attackers to ensure that the defender is reacting.

The defender is forced away from the second attacker:

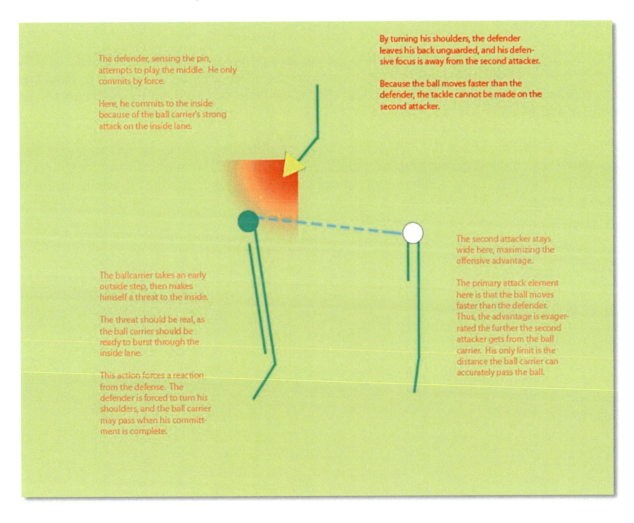

Additional Notes - Ruining Offensive Advantage with Spoilers:

Spoiler – Drifting

A true spoiler of a good pin is where the ball carrier runs, or "drifts", towards the outside lane and towards his own support player. In this situation, if there is no pressure from any other defender, it is a recipe for disaster. Why is this?

The advantage that is lost is the threat to the inside, and the distance the ball could travel that would outpace the defending man. If the ball carrier is not a threat to the inside, then there is no reason for the defender to stay near the inside lane, and no distance between him and the second attacker.

The result is typically that the ball carrier allows the defender to be in a physical space close to where both the ball carrier and the support player are. This increases the chances that the defender can physically address both attackers at once, because the attackers share the same space.

Here, the attacker makes an error when he chooses to pin the defender, but takes no initiative against the defender, either in speed or direction change:

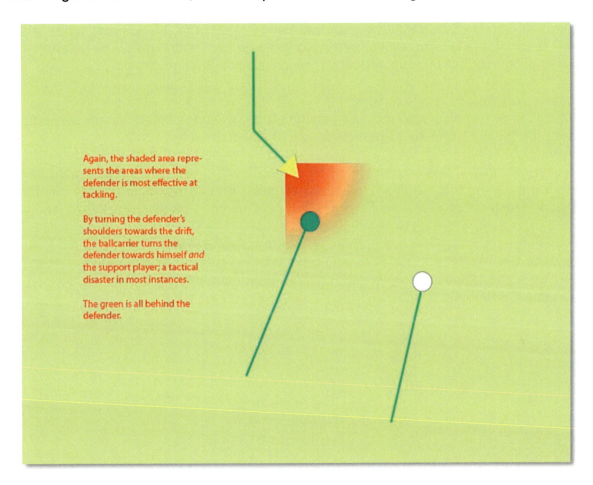

Again, the shaded area represents the areas where the defender is most effective at tackling.

By turning the defender's shoulders towards the drift, the ballcarrier turns the defender towards himself *and* the support player; a tactical disaster in most instances.

The green is all behind the defender.

Spoiler - Slow Movement by Ball carrier

The ball carrier can also spoil the action by his own malaise. If you slowly perform a tactic, you lose. All advantages in rugby are temporary.

As the ball carrier slows below his standard speed of 80-90%, his support slows, and the attack slows. By running to slow, there is no threat to the inside lane. The defender has a better chance to drift to the support player, successfully defending the play.

Spoiler - Soft Angles

The ball carrier can also spoil a pin by taking soft angles to the inside, or not varying attack speed after the cut – forfeiting two of elements of a good attack.

The best example of this is where the ball carrier fails to make "lane separation" from the defender, meaning that he does not get to an open lane to run through and still has the defender directly in front of him. The ball carrier is thus not a threat to the inside lane.

The primary reason that this is a problem is that the defender will not be obligated to turn his shoulders, leaving the support man within his tackling range, as the diagram shows. The defender in this situation can just wait until the right moment and drift to the support man, covering a greater deal of space.

Pinning in Three versus Two & Four versus Three Scenarios

Many players get discombobulated when additional attackers and defenders are added to the pinning scenario. This can be remedied. The key is to (1) understand which defender is the target of the attack, and (2) leave time for the pin on the target. The pin is still the goal.

This often time leaves a player with the conflicting goals of committing their defender and getting the ball out quickly. If the pass is made too soon, then the defenders can shift down to the next lane and compensate for the overload. If it is made too late, the ball is spoiled before it reaches the last attacker's hands, meaning, a tackle occurs before the pin can be made on the target defender.

The early movement of the ball carrier is thus key, and identical in purpose to the ball carrier in the two on one pin: force the defender's commitment to the inside lane, even if for a split second.

An offense should favor pinning when it has both greater numbers to the outside and ample space. While it is possible to win some situations through a scissor-pin, discussed later, it is oftentimes more efficient to pin the opposing players by relying more on ball speed and less player fitness to break the tackle line. Accordingly, in wide spaces, passing the ball down the line after noticing a numerical advantage is the most efficient attack.

In a three versus two scenario, the first movement and the spacing is nearly all that matters, setting the first defender to his lane, and leaving room to pin the final attacker:

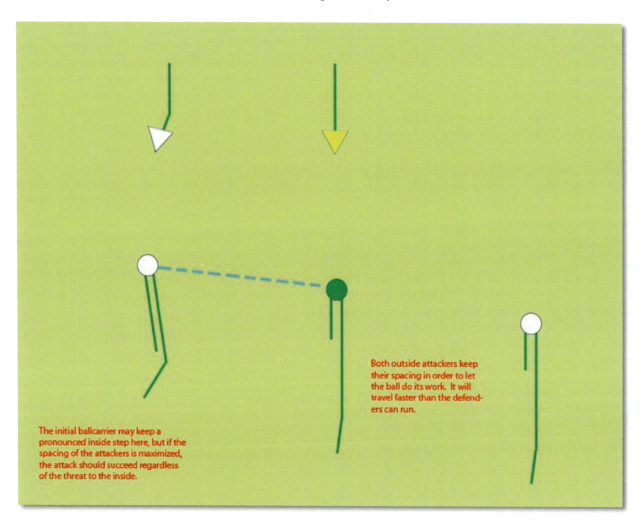

In a four versus three scenario, this can be done twice to isolate the third defender, who is then helpless to the pin. However, attackers should always favor the use of ball speed first. That means that if an outside overload exists, the attackers should prioritize passing, and make committing the defenders a secondary concern.

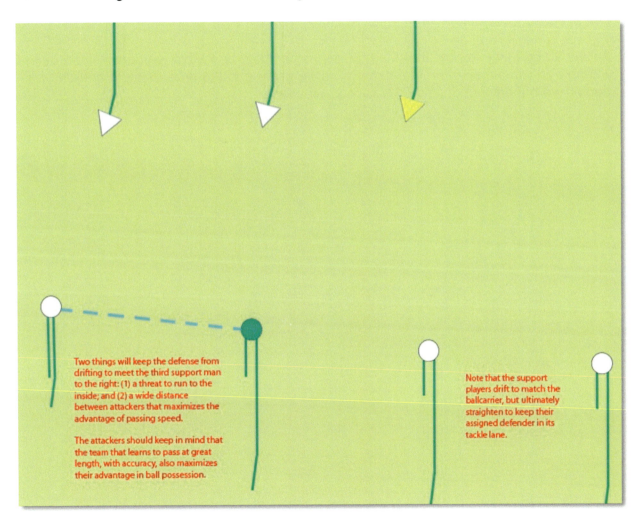

Two things will keep the defense from drifting to meet the third support man to the right: (1) a threat to run to the inside; and (2) a wide distance between attackers that maximizes the advantage of passing speed.

The attackers should keep in mind that the team that learns to pass at great length, with accuracy, also maximizes their advantage in ball possession.

Note that the support players drift to match the ballcarrier, but ultimately straighten to keep their assigned defender in its tackle lane.

Spoiler – Tight Offensive Alignments

If the offense keeps a tight alignment and does not use all available space, the defense will have its best opportunity to "push" to the outside attackers to defend against an outside advantage. Put another way, by lining up tight, the offense limits the advantage of ball speed; that the ball moves faster than the defenders.

This is a good time to note that the offensive advantage is always temporary – the defense will always compensate for its defensive flaws, given enough time. A tight backline attack decreases the amount of time for a successful attack.

Here, the backline is tight and the pass is made early, so the defense has adjusted:

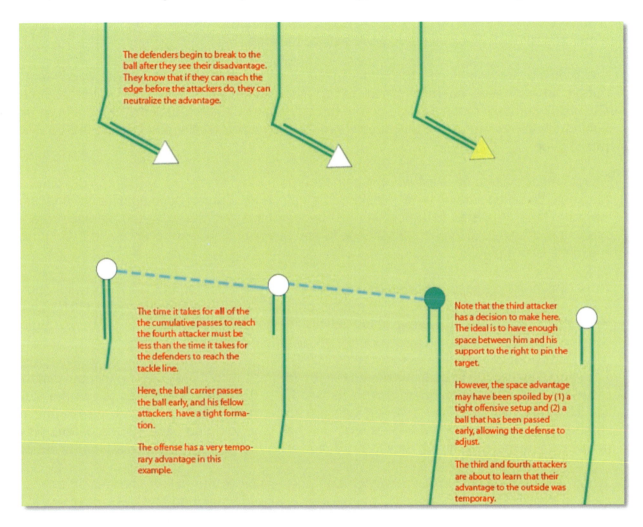

Spoiler – The Late Pass

Even when a numerical advantage exists and the offense is properly spaced, the initial ball carrier can ruin an attack by holding the ball for too long.

This problem presents itself in structured play when a flyhalf sees an outside overload in a four on three situation, but runs forward to commit the defense, only to have the defense meet his outside center to make a tackle before the advantage can be realized. It occurs in smaller pinning situations where the ball carrier simply does not trust his pass, holds the ball, and gets tackled.

Players must make a decision when it comes to both structured play and open field play – to pass outside *or* legitimately attack inside. The ball carrier cannot accomplish both attacks at the same time. Any step to the inside must be to set the defense only, and nothing more. Its overuse is ornamental and is a disservice to any attacking line, especially those that number in excess of two players.

Thus, a flyhalf that sees a field-wide advantage off a lineout, scrum, ruck, or maul should favor passing immediately, even if it means doing so from a standstill position. The flyhalf must know that there is a diminishing advantage to running towards the defense before passing the ball if doing so would sacrifice an outside overload.

The lineout leaves the largest cushion to run forward because it provides a minimum distance of twenty meters between the offensive backline and the defense, the position of the tackle line changes. Accordingly, a flyhalf can run forward to create an inside threat and not immediately jeopardize his outside threat. He has time to do so because the defense is so far away. The more the flyhalf runs forward, however, the less time is left to attack the outside.

When a scrum, ruck, or maul produces ball possession to the flyhalf, there is little time or need to suggest an inside attack. The defense is already matched and does not need to be manipulated further. A flyhalf running towards the tackle line in these instances actually diminishes the chance of pinning the outside, target defender.

In short, attackers must realize an outside advantage quickly by acting immediately, and that means favoring the pass to an inside threat.

The Scissor / Switch — Against a Single, Misaligned Defender

A second method to win a two versus one is the scissor, also known as a switch. It capitalizes on poor defensive positioning and an extreme change in speed and direction by the ball carrier. The scissor allows the ball carrier to offload to a support player who crosses from the outside lane to the inside lane:

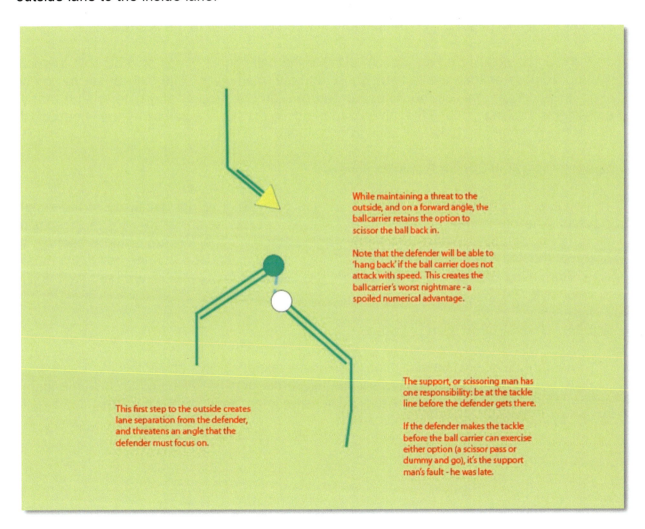

The ball carrier takes an early cut at burst to either create lane separation or at least threaten a breakaway on the outside lane. The move forces commitment by the defender and forces the defender to pursue and turn his shoulders to the ball carrier. The ball carrier can then dump the ball off to the cutting support player.

Note that both players must be running at their burst well prior to the tackle line.

This should be considered an "option" play for the ball carrier - he should be able to decide whether to pass or keep the ball and go, a "dummy" maneuver. The ball carrier, having two eyes, should keep one on the defender and one on his support player to ensure that the defender is tracking him and that an offload needs to occur. The ball carrier can then pop the ball at the proper time, or keep it and go.

Spoiler - The Ball Carrier Runs Backward

The sure way to ruin a scissor attack is for the ball carrier to run backward to the support players. The ball carrier should always keep an "attack" angle, or forward facing posture towards the defense, even if just a few degrees' angle. The forward angle preserves the option of the ball carrier to, if the defender stays in the inside lane, run the ball to the outside lane after faking the pass. We will explore the fake or dummy pass more later as it applies to defensive weaknesses.

Spoiler - The Support Man is Late

The support man should keep in mind that it is his responsibility - and solely his responsibility - to get to the tackle line in time before the ball carrier gets hit. Remember, the time that the support man possesses to get the tackle line is equal to, if not slightly less than, the time the defender will take to get to the ball carrier.

Chapter 2, Section 2
Attacking Defects in the Defense

If the game were only about counting how many players were on a particular area of the pitch, it probably would not be very exciting.

The reality is that good defenses minimize numerical disadvantages, and in many situations on the field completely eliminate them, such as in set plays near the goal line. All other numbers being equal then, the offense must find another way to use the elements of advantage to break the tackle line.

When numbers are equal, the offense must look for defects in the defensive line. Defects are by definition a weakness. In rugby, they can be defined as a defensive posture that decreases the defense's chance to tackle the ball carrier at the tackle line or otherwise prevent beneficial movement of the ball across the pitch.

Three common defects exist:
1. Alignment – One or more defensive tackle lanes are not lined up laterally over the attackers.
2. Width – Defensive tackle lanes are outside of the distance between two attackers, leaving inside space.
3. Staggering – Defensive front is not "flat" at the tackle line, leaving angled windows of attack.

While defenses are also weakened because of talent, skill level, or physical characteristics, those attributes will always be addressed in relation to the other three factors. After all, a defensive player who is limited in any one of those physical attributes can still properly align themselves, make proper spacing, and eliminate staggering.

Put another way, physical attributes of individual defense players are certainly relevant, but are most important and analyzable, for purposes of this book, when *those individual player attributes have caused or can cause some <u>other</u> defect in the defense.*

The Bounce - *Against Misaligned Defenses*

A typical defensive weakness is a misalignment, whereby the defenders are not lined up over their offensive counterparts. This is a situation where lane separation has already occurred or can easily occur for the attacker.

The "bounce" is a maneuver to the outside that exploits this defensive weakness. It can be employed if the (1) the ball carrier has created lane separation to the outside of his assigned defender; (2) the offensive support player is fast enough to maintain near-equality with the ball carrier; and (3) the offensive support will not reach the sideline before the ball carrier reaches the tackle line (ie: the play won't run out of bounds before it is successful).

Alternately, a misalignment can be forced when a fleet-footed back encounters a flat-footed forward. That backline player may be able to create a misalignment by breaking hard to his opposing defender's outside, and can be successful if his cut is sharply angled and speed burst properly applied.

In either scenario, the bounce tactic actually changes the count of the matchup, artificially creating an outside overload and giving the offense an advantage even when the number of defenders was initially equal to the number of attackers.

The bounce can create a pin opportunity to the outside:

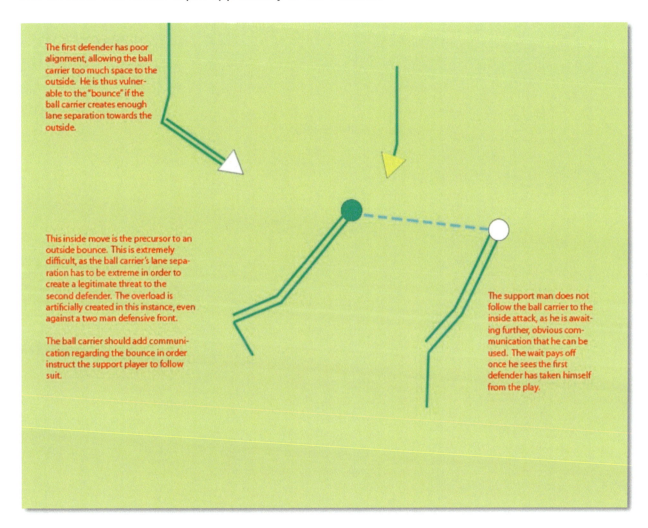

The bounce can also create a change in numerical superiority in a three on two situation:

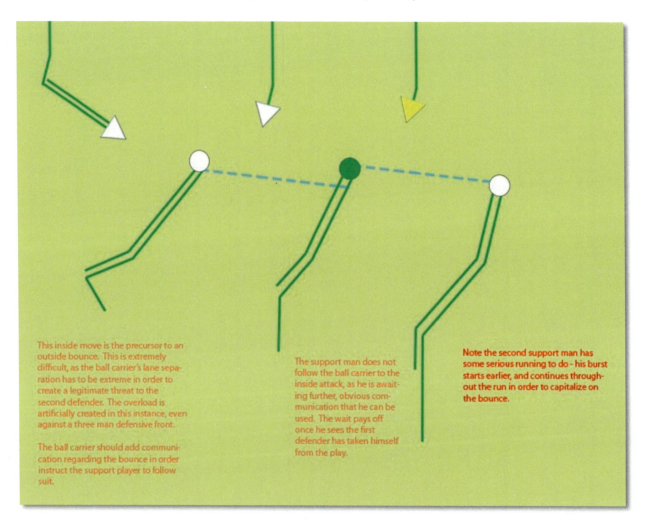

This inside move is the precursor to an outside bounce. This is extremely difficult, as the ball carrier's lane separation has to be extreme in order to create a legitimate threat to the second defender. The overload is artificially created in this instance, even against a three man defensive front.

The ball carrier should add communication regarding the bounce in order instruct the support player to follow suit.

The support man does not follow the ball carrier to the inside attack, as he is awaiting further, obvious communication that he can be used. The wait pays off once he sees the first defender has taken himself from the play.

Note the second support man has some serious running to do - his burst starts earlier, and continues throughout the run in order to capitalize on the bounce.

This second example is possible but is the rarest, as it requires extreme athleticism from all support players that accompany the ball carrier. It starts with the ball carrier, though, who must have an athleticism that matches or exceeds his peers on both defense and offense.

In either of the above examples, the situation can be won by the offense even if one of the sliding defensive players attempt to play soft (or even run backward) in an attempt to give the trailing defender time to catch the ball carrier.

As in the crash, shown later, the ball carrier simply needs to "ride the back" of the remaining defender, using the space behind him, shown here as a green rectangle:

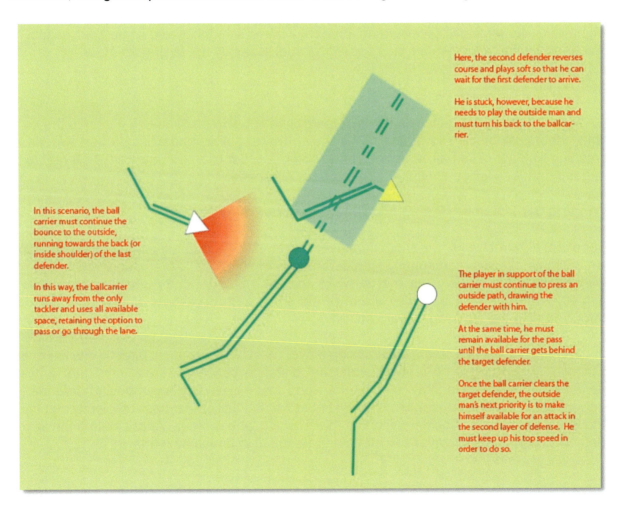

The Crash - *Against Wide and Staggered Defenses of Equal Number*

A crash is designed to break the tackle line when there are equal numbers of attackers and defenders.

There is no numerical advantage in a crash, so a crash might be considered an inside pin of sorts that must account for a second defender who has wide or staggered defensive alignment. Nonetheless, if executed properly, the crash takes an angle that cannot be defended by the late defender, and cannot be addressed by the target defender.

Setting the Crash

On seeing a staggered defense, the ball carrier can set a crash by taking action to the inside lane, then straightening to attack. This draws the target defender inside and widens the crashing window. The ball carrier must straighten in order to create a legitimate threat to the target defender's inside shoulder, and attack at full speed.

Winning the Crash by Seeing and Breaking the Window

For a crash to truly work, the crashing player must understand that the concepts of the tackle line become skewed momentarily. If a defender is out of place, either staggered or wide, he will be late to his tackle. The line on which the late defender can make a tackle becomes angled, is not flat, and becomes a tool of the offense; it represents a "plane" or "window" through which the crashing player can run.

In order to succeed in a crash, the crashing player must be ready to cut directly into the angled window. In doing so, he creates additional distance between himself and the opposing defender. The crashing player should not worry that by evading his opposing defender, he gets closer to the target defender. He must trust that the ball carrier has sufficiently committed the target defender's shoulders and that the crashing lane is clear. After clearing the second defender, the crashing player can straighten up the field for his next attack.

Crashing windows on the rugby pitch have three common characteristics (1) they are open temporarily; (2) they are not typically flat against the field; and (3) they are meant to be crashed through at full speed.

A crash is appropriate against staggered defenses of equal number:

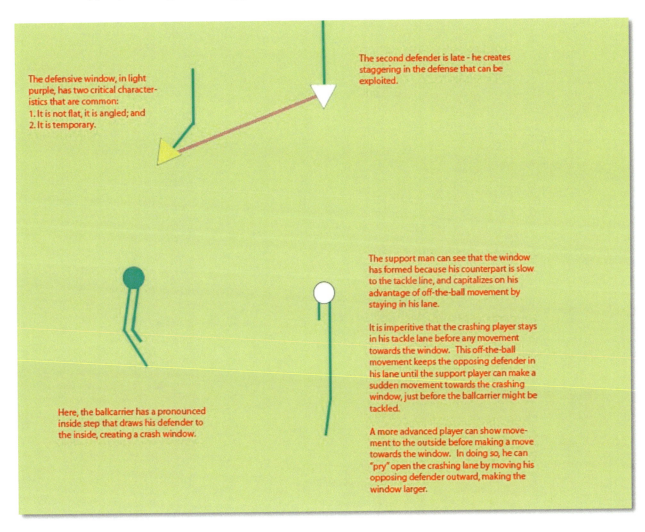

A crashing player must hit the window perpendicular to its plane. Doing so produces the most desirable result, as it is the furthest distance from his defender, is on the opposite side of the target defender, and leaves room to crash even further to the inside:

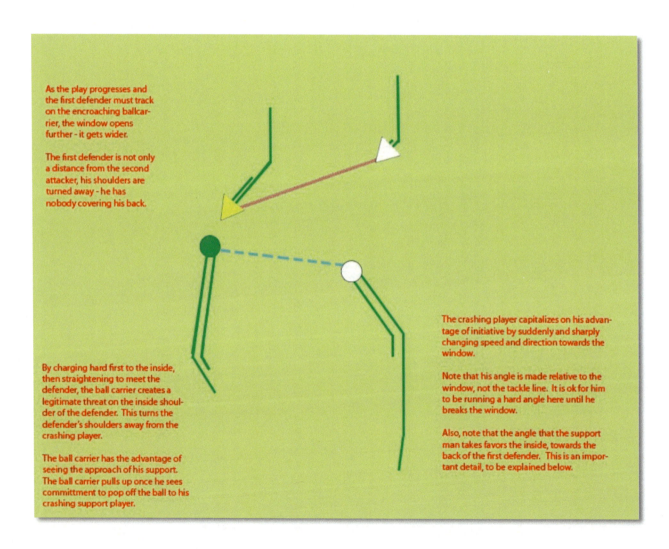

After the attacker breaks through the window, he must run up the field and maintain forward momentum. It will most certainly be the path of least resistance to the try zone and the location of the next layer of defense:

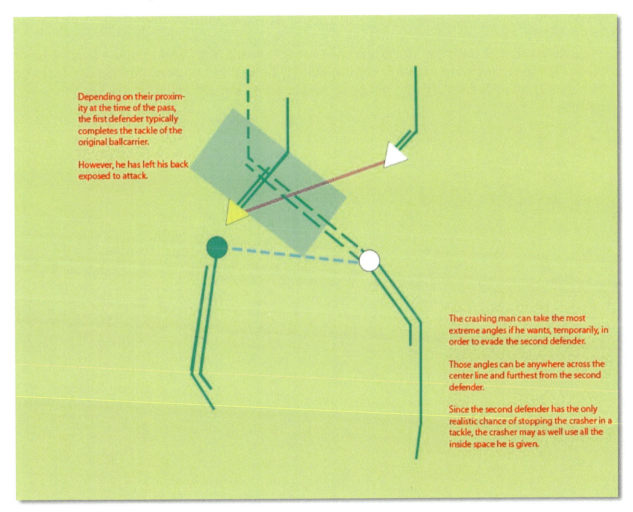

Using the Space behind the Target Defender

The reality that most crashers will find is that, if they look closely, there is an abundance of space *behind* the target defender on a crash, just as there was on the outside defender during the bounce.

Because the target defender does not have arms that are designed to make tackles behind his back, the crasher can theoretically run directly behind the back of the first defender until he clears the tackle line - "riding his back" until he can straighten up to the second layer of defense:

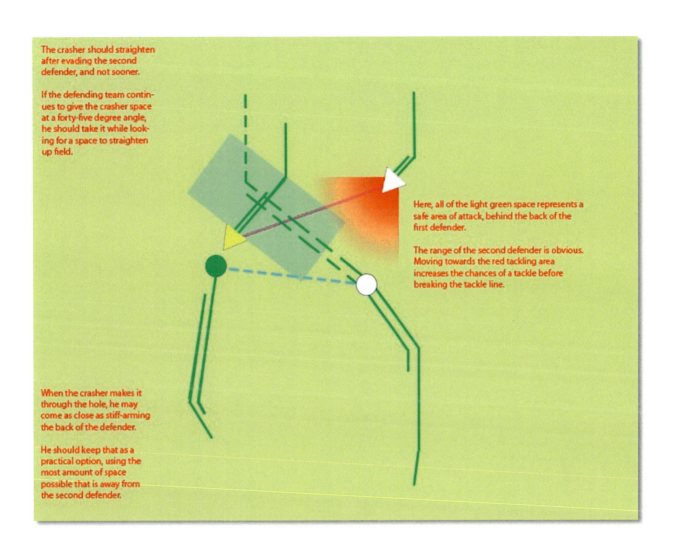

The Dummy Scissor - *Against Staggered Defenses of Equal Number*

When the first defender is overzealous and attacks the outside lane too quickly, this changes the use of the scissor attack. The unevenness creates a different opportunity - allowing the ball carrier to exploit the tendencies of the defense during a scissor move.

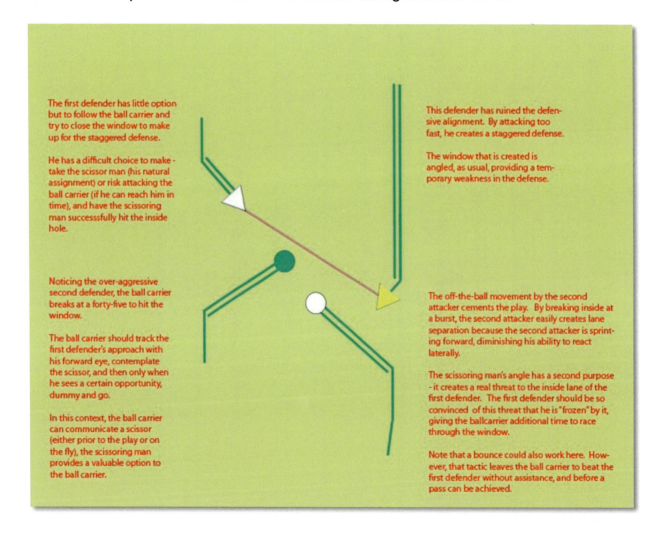

The first defender has little option but to follow the ball carrier and try to close the window to make up for the staggered defense.

He has a difficult choice to make - take the scissor man (his natural assignment) or risk attacking the ball carrier (if he can reach him in time), and have the scissoring man successsfully hit the inside hole.

Noticing the over-aggressive second defender, the ball carrier breaks at a forty-five to hit the window.

The ball carrier should track the first defender's approach with his forward eye, contemplate the scissor, and then only when he sees a certain opportunity, dummy and go.

In this context, the ball carrier can communicate a scissor (either prior to the play or on the fly), the scissoring man provides a valuable option to the ball carrier.

This defender has ruined the defensive alignment. By attacking too fast, he creates a staggered defense.

The window that is created is angled, as usual, providing a temporary weakness in the defense.

The off-the-ball movement by the second attacker cements the play. By breaking inside at a burst, the second attacker easily creates lane separation because the second attacker is sprinting forward, diminishing his ability to react laterally.

The scissoring man's angle has a second purpose - it creates a real threat to the inside lane of the first defender. The first defender should be so convinced of this threat that he is "frozen" by it, giving the ballcarrier additional time to race through the window.

Note that a bounce could also work here. However, that tactic leaves the ball carrier to beat the first defender without assistance, and before a pass can be achieved.

Here, the over-pursuit of an outside man creates an inside window to exploit. As the scissoring player and the ball carrier cross paths, the first defender (who is in position) is left with a Hobbesian choice to cover one of two lanes. If the offensive player keeps an eye on which lane the first defender commits to, he can either complete the scissor or effectuate the dummy through the window:

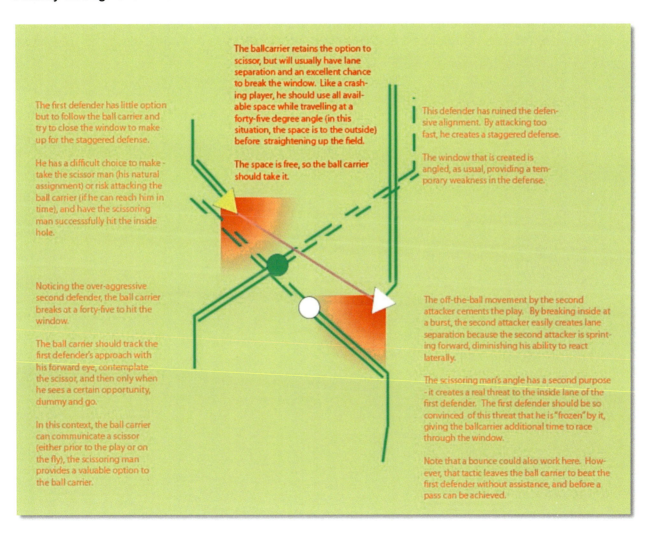

Just as in a traditional crash, the dummying ball carrier can break the window, having the same option to attack space behind the second defender.

Once through the tackle line, the attacker has many possibilities, including an opening for an attack on the second layer of defense that can produce a score, a substantial change in field position, or momentum change. Either way, the dummy should be used a deadly attack on an uneven defense. A team's backline attack strategy, in fact, should deign to use this to break the tackle line on a consistent basis.

The Loop - *Against Wide and Staggered Defenses of Equal Number*

Often construed as a way to produce an outside overload on a section of the defense, the loop best functions to capitalize on unevenness in the defensive line. It exerts pressure on the inside first.

The loop can be used to provide support to an attack, as in the second phase. However, it should not cause an outside overload because, as the ball carrier gives up the ball, the defender who previously covered him switches his assignment to the support man who received the pass, and a second defender slides to the outside. This is a common and necessary defensive adjustment.

Thus, the looping player's movement is entirely predictable to his new, defensive opponent. Since the new defender is outside of the looper, the looper cannot create lane separation to the outside because he is travelling to the inside of the new defender's lane. The defensive assignment has him covered.

What happens, however, is that the defense is sometimes tricked or habituated to over-pursue the supporting attackers on the outside, forgetting the looping man on the inside.

Defensive over-pursuit creates a window for the looping man to crash through along the way:

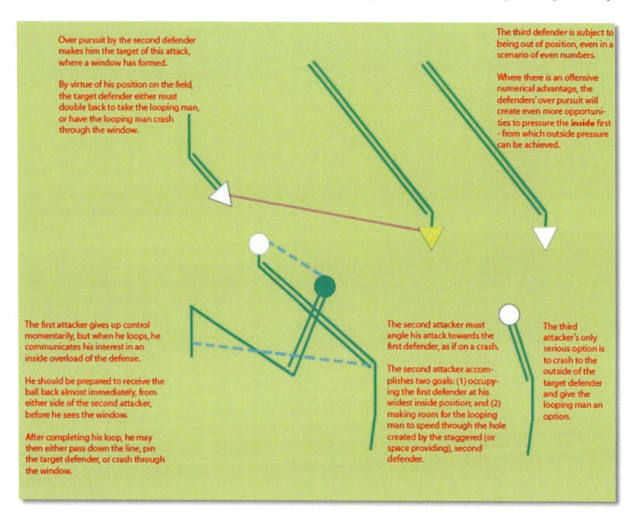

Note that the window in this example is at the same angle that is typically available in a bounce attack.

Break the Line – Analysis & Method

The ball carrier faces pressure from the second defender immediately after making a movement to insert himself back into the line of attack, so he should change his speed and direction drastically towards the window. After receiving the ball, the looping ball carrier should break directly through the window:

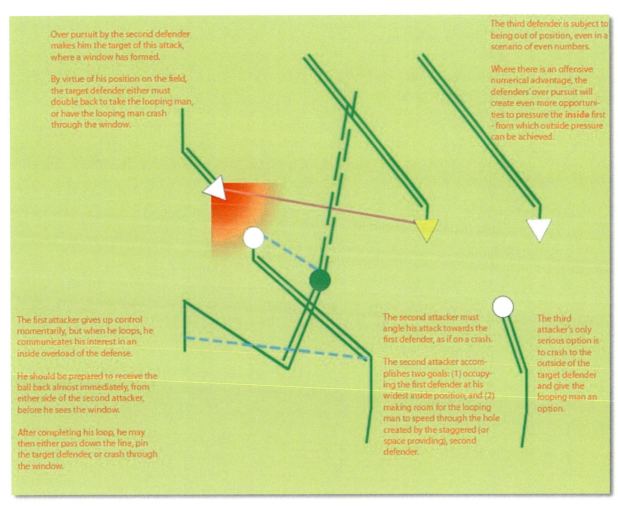

In this and all of the tactics in this chapter, the offense excels by using the elements of attack. Each of the movements in the loop require the offense, especially the looping man, to apply its mastery of initiative. The looping playing changes the speed and direction of play throughout this tactic, and must do so in a way that is both extreme and not at all obvious to the defense.

The loop exemplifies the difficulty in mastering all of the elements from the first chapter, because the offense is forced to make so many deceptive movements through the tactic. It shows us that each change in speed and direction can mean the difference between being tackled and breaking the tackle line.

That is the larger theme in all attacking: Without dedication to fundamentals - the elements - the lines on the diagrams of the tactics are worthless. Communication must be established, off-the-ball positioning and movement must be precise, ball speed must be sharp, initiative must be seized, and changes in speed and direction must be extreme, or the tactics fail.

The third section of this chapter will show why this is true, as in that section, the defense will be at no cognizable disadvantage in number or posture *except* to be subject to those very fundamental elements.

Chapter 2, Section 3
Combo Tactics – Creating Defects in the Defense

Now that we've observed each of the tactics that derive from the elements in Chapter 1, as well as the movements in sections one and two of this chapter, we can accept some additional truths:
1. The defense must react in predictable ways; and
2. A combination of tactics can be used to force that predictability.

In chess, placing your opponent in a position of forced movement is called "zugzwang," which translated from German is "compulsion to move." Your opponent should have no choice but to make a bad choice. Your opponent cannot chose to forfeit his move. Consequently, you can force the opponent to move into trouble.

The game of rugby is not much different - it is about creating an advantage in time, space, structure, and power. There are no squares, but the capabilities of each player can be distilled to a known quantity in space and time. Where mastery of the application of power is a necessary discipline of any forward, the mastery of time and space by initiative, ball speed, and off-the-ball movement must be the craft of every backline player. As in chess, mastering the timing and the space of play can be just as effective as the application of power in winning any given game.

Consequently, the tactics in this section maximize the exploitation of time and space to win a particular situation.

The intent is to later work the combination tactics from open field play into a strategy that anticipates structured play, with set piece attacks, as we will discuss in chapter three. The combinations in this section become the basis for plays that are called after reading defensive alignments, and work directly into any offensive plan.

The Scissor Pin – *For Numerical Advantages in Tight Spaces*

The scissor-pin is an excellent example of capitalizing on zugzwang, where the defense is forced to make a bad move and the offense retains all options to make a good move.

The scissor-pin is a combo movement that includes a scissor followed by a pin, and is applied to situations in which three attackers encounter two defenders, but passing down the line might be a bad idea. In tight space, attackers simply may not have the time to pass down the line and guarantee a win to the outside against a defense that either shifts quickly to the outside, or plays "soft" by backpedaling as far as possible and feigning tackles so as to draw a bad pass.

This substitute, combination attack should produce a significant offense advantage, even in tighter spaces along the sidelines, because of the way the tactic forces bad defensive decisions. This tactic should be used whenever possible.

By this movement, the ball carrier creates four options: a possible scissor, dummy, pin, or bounce.

Each results in a win.

Option 1: When the first defender defends the scissoring player, and the second defender defends the ball carrier on the switch, it opens up the pin:

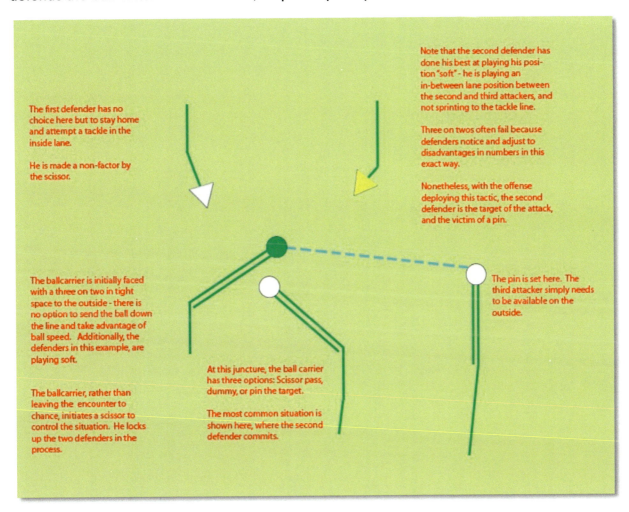

Option 2: When the second defender takes the outside man, the ball carrier can keep on the dummy scissor:

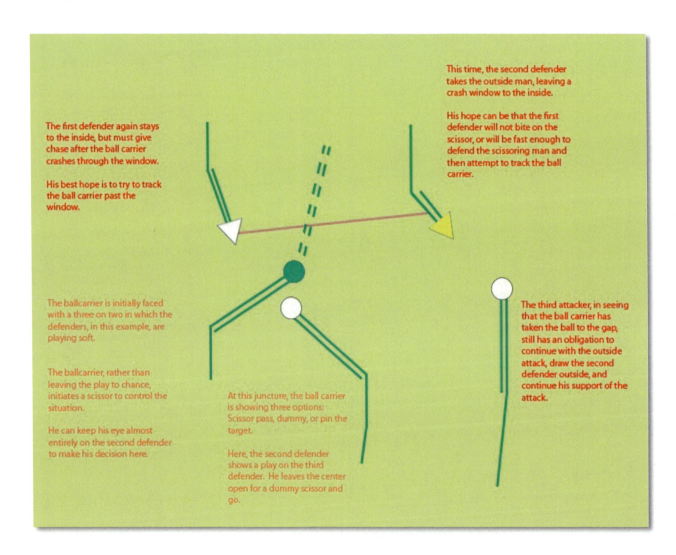

Option 3: When the first defender stays on the ball carrier, the ball carrier passes off to the scissoring support.

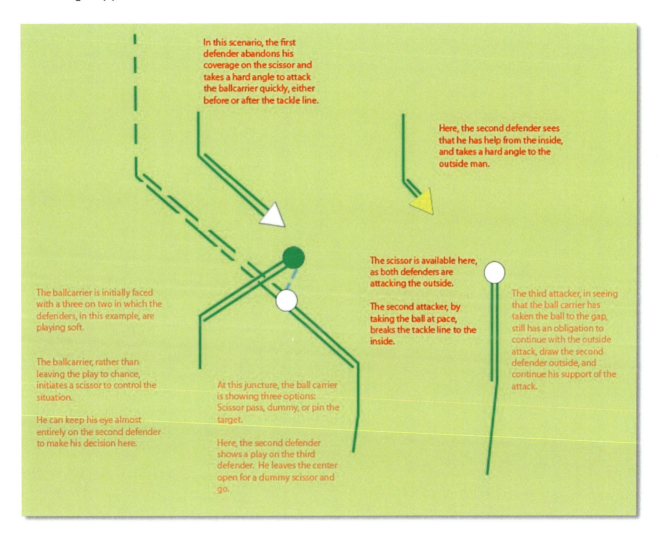

Option 4: When the first defender plays soft on the scissor, the ball carrier bounces to the outside defender, taking an aggressive angle behind the target defender.

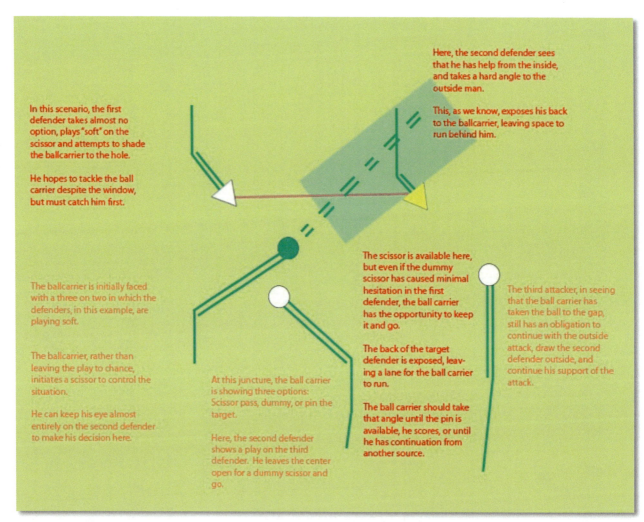

You might say, why not just pass it down the line? There a numerous reasons. The first of which is that a three man attack in open field is a subject to extreme variability. Even the best ball carriers will spoil a three versus two opportunity by passing too quickly and allowing the

Break the Line – Analysis & Method

defense to shift to the outside attackers. Another is that it is difficult for the ball carrier to perceive whether there is enough space to create an outside attack. The other is that passing down the line involves two passes, while the scissor-pin requires just one to break the tackle line – there is less of a chance for a knock on or errant pass attempt.

Primarily the scissor-pin should be the preferred method of attack because a ball carrier does not always have time to check the first defender and force him to the inside lane. The scissoring player forces this to happen for the attacking side. As we discussed on the section regarding the dummy move, the first defender is forced to make a Hobbesian choice to tackle the ball carrier or cover the inside lane, but cannot do both.

Having acted first, and with burst, the attackers can establish the initiative before any of the lanes can be covered. The scissor man and the support player should both anticipate this maneuver once the numerical advantage is realized, and once the ball carrier makes this first move. The communication, change in speed, change in direction, and ball flight should produce a winning result in every encounter.

Additional Notes:

Spoiler – Late Scissoring
The unforced error that is typically made with this sure-fire combo tactic is a late attempt to scissor. A ball carrier risks ruining his opportunity for the pin when he approaches the tackle line for any more time that is absolutely necessary.

A late scissor creates a flatter scissoring angle. This leaves the ball carrier with a less aggressive line towards the defense. Some ball carriers go so far as to run *backwards* because their scissor attempt was so late. This is typically disastrous. Second, a late scissor attempt creates a flatter pass to the outside man, by necessity. This is a harder pass to make, and with a flatter attack angle, the defender can keep a hand in the passing lane and reach the pass. Third, a late scissor adds time pressure on the offense to either pass or go. All three effects need to be avoided.

The Scissor Crash – *Against Even Numbers and a Flat Defense*

The scissor crash is not much different, but can be used when the offense and defense are equally matched - three attackers approach three defenders, one of the most difficult offensive approaches in rugby.

Because there are even numbers between the offense and the defense, three on each side in this example, the offense must act quickly and decisively to *create* advantage. This means sharp changes in speed and direction that create an opportunity for the offense in what otherwise looks like a stalemate. A disciplined backline should not feel lost here; it has weapons that exploit all of the above observations in the attacking game.

In situations with equal numbers, all four elements must be emphasized to create a win:
1. Communication
2. Off-the-Ball Positioning and Movement
3. Initiative
4. Ball Speed

Applying these elements puts the defense out of position to handle a well-timed attack, because each player understands the plan with prior communication, is properly aligned off the ball, changes both speed and direction in an extreme way, and is ready to dispense the ball quickly, even in tight space.

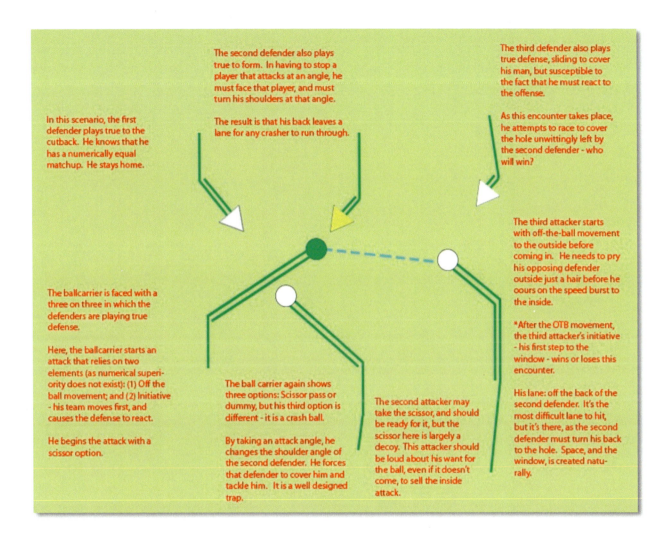

By virtue of the dummy scissor, the second defender must turn his shoulders to the support man on the outside. With some off the ball movement, the support player can become a crasher - he can ride the back of the second defender through the tackle line, running away from the third defender in the process:

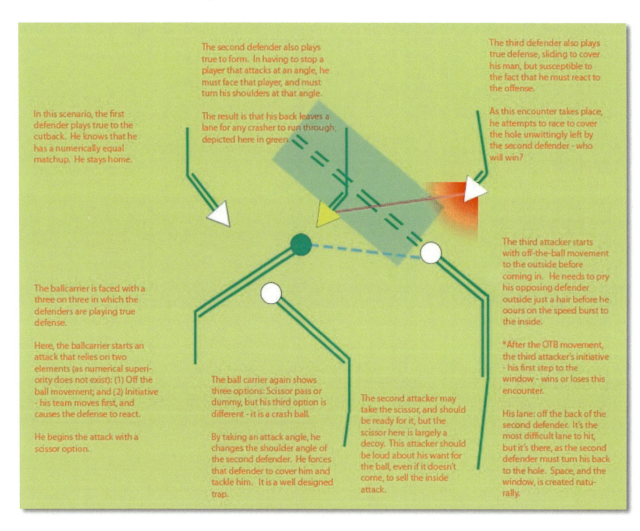

The offensive win is possible because the third defender is forced to take an outside tact at the beginning of the sequence, and cannot track back fast enough to close the window.

The window is pried open further by virtue of the scissor attack. The second defender widens the window because he must turn his shoulders and step inside to cover the ball carrier. The second defender, having turned to cover his assignment, cannot react fast enough to turn and tackle the crashing player.

Variation – Scissor & Bounce

One variation can occur if the second defender plays tight to the first defender, sharing his lane. The ball carrier then could dummy scissor, separate from the second defender, and bounce to the outside. This would create an outside attack against the third defender, who then stands alone in defense. The pin should then be automatic.

Variation – Loop & Crash

A variation can be run of this with a loop, rather than a scissor, at its beginning. However, the speed of the ball carrier can be an issue. In the scissor crash, the ball carrier takes a hard angle and causes commitment from an appreciable speed. This is not true for a loop, which creates a softer angle and slower development.

Chapter 3
Applying the Tactics to Structured Gameplay

All of the tactics in this book can be used in structured play, and all have been translated into plays in the backline, used every day by clubs around the world.

The key for any backline is to keep all of the stuff that makes the tactics work, but be able to run those tactics in a backline from breakdowns and set pieces. All of the above can and should be applied in the loose, but a great deal more success can come from having predictable defensive setups, with defenders at a standstill, with clean ball from the scrumhalf, and with a play dialed-up and ready to execute.

After all, an offense's communication advantage is at its highest when it can call a secret play.

But the reality is that a backline tends to become mechanical when it runs plays, losing all of the magic that makes open field plays so dynamic. Why is that? Because the play is contrived, the players run the play repeatedly and lazily at practice, and/or the ideas about initiative, ball speed, and movement become lost. Ideas about the tackle line are confused. Speed changes occur slowly, and nothing is a surprise to the defense. The backline becomes a liability to the team.

In many ways, that's why this book was written.

Poor application of tactic commonly happens with the 1-2 crash, where the flyhalf dumps a pass to the inside center. If planned poorly, the play is destined to fail - the defense can see it unfold, no initiative is taken, and the offense dooms itself by a predictable approach to the tackle line. Without the nuance of all the tactics, the crash between the FH and IC is wasted.

That can all be changed by developing plays that focus on attacking a particular target, just as diagrammed in Chapter 2, and using the elements of attack from Chapter 1.

So here's a good breakdown of common plays and their translation to this book:

1. 1-2 Crash – Crash between FH and IC
2. 1-3 Crash – Scissor Crash using FH, IC and OC
3. 1-5 Crash – Scissor Crash using FH and FB, after a Dummy Scissors with the IC, OC, or both.
4. 1-2 Scissor – Scissor between FH and pack, or FH and IC (depending on weakness).
5. 1-3 Scissor – Dummy Scissor between the FH and IC followed by a Scissor between FH & OC.
6. 1-2 Loop – Loop Crash between the FH and IC
7. Skip – Outside Attack which hopefully ends in a Crash by the OC and FB or a Pin for the FB and SSW

The next step in application is being able to choose which play to run, even with this very basic playset. When a defensive backline is set, what should compel one play to be called over the other?

The answer is: The play that employs the tactic that will win.

If there is no obvious defensive weakness, the answer is to create such a weakness by creating an expectation, then defying it. This considers the elements from an offense-wide, strategic viewpoint. After an expectation is built about the speed and direction of play, for example, the offense then can then run movements that counter that speed and direction to create a successful attack.

Reading the Defense - *Analytically Breaking Down a Defense*

One of the most overwhelming problems a flyhalf faces is seeing the field, or "reading the defense."

The flyhalf must make command decisions on the field in order to apply tactics, but doing so can be difficult because there are so many people on the field at the same time. The flyhalf simplifies this process for the ground attack by focusing on those players that can reach the tackle line and defend against his backline, and by counting those defenders against the number of attackers available to him:

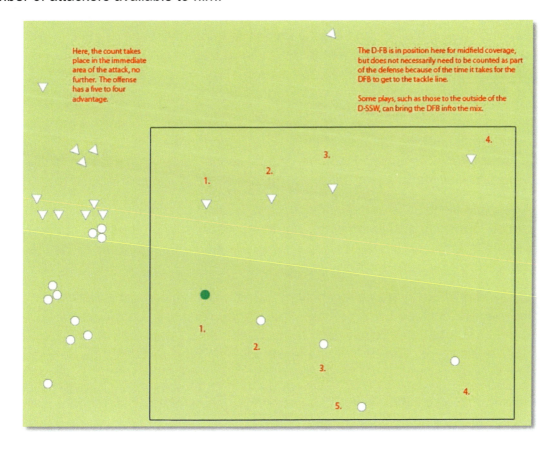

Break the Line – Analysis & Method

After examining those players in position to make a play on the tackle line, the flyhalf can then then "read" the field to guide how to attack using the tactics.

Three reads are necessary to do so: (1) A read of each individual defensive player's skills and abilities, (2) a read of the set position of the defense prior to touching or as touching the ball; and (3) remembering the historical actions of the defense in order to exploit them, taking into account numbers (1) and (2).

1. **Reading Your Opponent's Abilities – Looking at them before whistle, during play, and for the whole match.**

The read of the individual athletes might include their height, weight, strength, speed, and tackling ability. This is the first and most common read of any coach or athlete. Who is the weak player on the other side? Where is the physical mismatch? Which opposing player is unseasoned in rugby, or a substitute for the starter? How can we exploit individuals to make defects in the defense?

This examination should not end at a pre-game peek of the opposing side's warmups or films. It continues throughout the entirety of the game, during loose play by the ball carrier, and after the breakdown if possible. Examine who looks lost, who is afraid, who is tired. All of that *looking* will help inform a play call.

In loose play, the decision to dummy or scissor or pin may be made by looking at the eyes of the defender. His body position may tell you that the player is on the field, but the eyes will reveal he has lost interest in play, or that his body can no longer perform. The instant read might change the attacker's decision making.

This can and should be done by every player, even those supporting the ball carrier. In doing so, those players can read the defense themselves, make tactical decisions when they become the ball carrier, and report good reads back to the flyhalf for use in the come plays: "The D-OC is slow," or "The SSW can't tackle me," or "The D-IC is huge, let's be sure to attack him at angles."

All of this information can be helpful if shared, even if some of it is disregarded. One thing is certain; it is useless if unobserved or kept secret.

2. Reading the Set Position of the Defense – Looking at them before they approach the tackle line.

A defense should be read based on its position on the field, which typically features the D-FB either set back in kick coverage or in the line. Because this book covers the ground attack exclusively, and does not discuss kicking tactics or strategies, we can simplify the common positions and considerations.

While outside defensive overloads can exist, we'll keep things simple here and assume standard defense, with man-to-man matchups.

Near their own 22 meter mark and at midfield, the offense retains the advantage of a D-FB that is dropped back in kick coverage. Two variations mark the typical backline Defense, the first of which is a wide D-SSW:

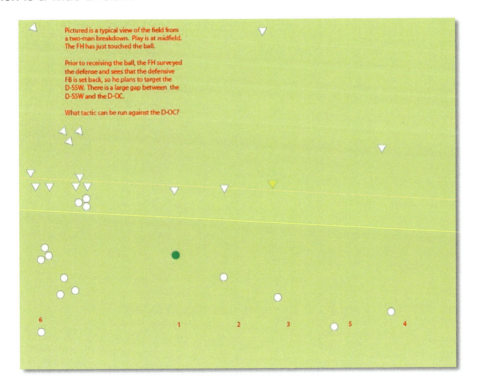

A second variation is the tight D-SSW:

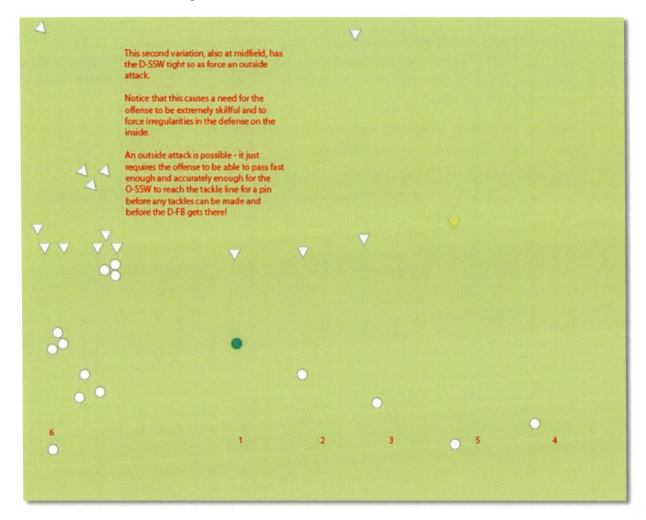

Reading either variation gives a flyhalf some information to work with.

A closer examination might reveal other gaps such as a gap, with misalignment, at the centers:

Or staggering at the centers:

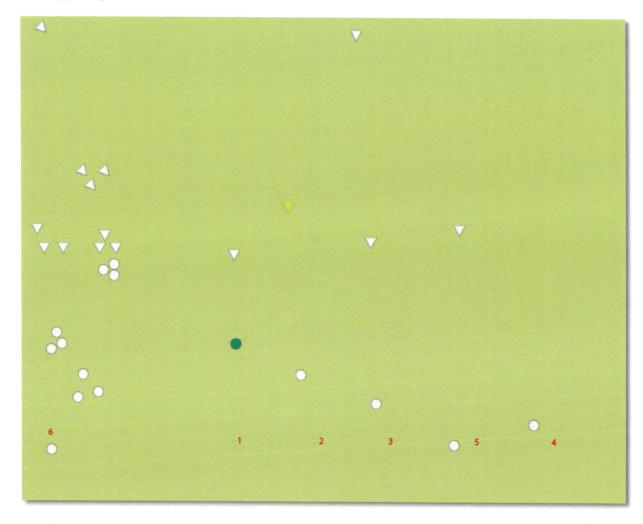

Or excess width between the D-FH and D-IC:

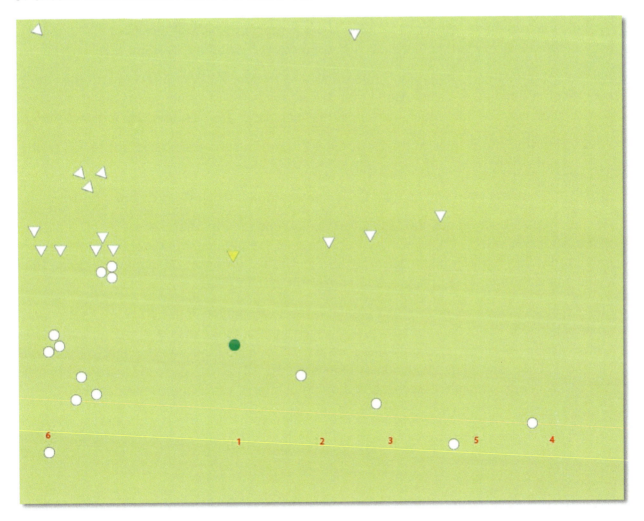

All of this makes for useful information that can be applied to a play call.

All of it can also inform the movements of the attackers as the play unfolds, based on where the defender started from. One can expect, for example, a D-FB to have to run at full speed to make the tackle line. This can limit the D-FB to making a difficult tackle, at full speed, and without the ability to change direction. Knowing the D-FB starting position reveals that.

As this setup changes throughout the period of a match, a savvy attacker can then notice how much a defense is compensating for the weaknesses of its individual athletes. And in combination with the third read, can examine which plays are best to call in a given moment.

3. Reading the Habits of the Defense – Examining the defensive approach to the tackle line.

The third defensive read occurs after the defense starts moving towards the offense.

As the defense approaches the tackle line, weakness may appear that were not noticeable in the defensive setup. Changes may also occur as the defense approaches. One defender might run wide. Another might approach too fast. Another might be lagging behind. These variations create gaps, staggering, and in general, opportunities.

One of the simplest ways to these weaknesses is to induce them. For example, calling several plays to the outside before calling several plays to the inside is a common method. Once a set of plays is attempted, they create reactions by the defense that will inevitably repeated. Once a weakness during any analysis exists, it can be made the focus of a backline attack for an entire match, if necessary, if no adjustments are made by the defense.

But every team, nearly, shows some sort of weakness by one of their players, in some sort of situation during the game.

A common weakness is the "cheating" center, looking for the big hit all game:

This over-aggressive approach creates a "window" as we know. The defense is staggered, and therefore weak enough to run through. A dummy scissor attempt at that position, either by the FH or the IC, and with the OC, would tear the line to shreds, getting the offense to the second line of defense.

What would be left would be a D-FB, waiting to be victim to a pin between the breakaway player and his support, either the FB or SSW.

Here's the window, just as we described it in prior chapters:

A dummy scissor by the IC, if not the FH (after dummying with the IC), crashes directly through it. Seeing that a D-OC does this on a regular basis gives a FH good information to act on.

This "aggressive" move can be made by the D-OC, the D-IC, or the D-FH, all creating different weaknesses for a defense. Look at what happens when the D-IC is foolish enough to do it to a watchful offense:

Here, the D-IC is the weakness, and two windows open for the offense to exploit. The defense's position is unrecoverable if the FH is prescient enough to run a dummy scissor with the IC. Even if the ball is cast beyond the D-IC on a skip pass, the defense even shows weakness back towards the inside. The D-OC is forced to play both to the inside and outside of his tackle lane, leaving him vulnerable.

These tendencies should be examined and re-evaluated through the course of a match. Halftime is an excellent time to discuss tendencies, but this can be accomplished during play as well. The key is to be *looking* for what your opponent is or is not doing.

The defense will inevitably show you its weakness – it cannot be hidden. Perhaps discovering it at the final minute of the match will be enough to give your team an edge.

Reading the Defense – *A First Example*

Imagine a match is in its fiftieth minute and your team has been making the three reads. You may use any of the tactics in this book to attack the defensive line, because your coach wants to keep the ball in hand.

Read type 1 – the defensive outside center is slower than the offensive outside center by several steps, even though he's an effective tackler.

Read type 2 – the line sets up tight at the centers, so as to stop inside attacks. The D-SSW sets up wide at midfield, moves to the inside to cover the gap, and allows the FB to fill to the outside.

Read type 3 – the defenders come up even, without deviating from the lanes they started in.

The situation typically develops like this:

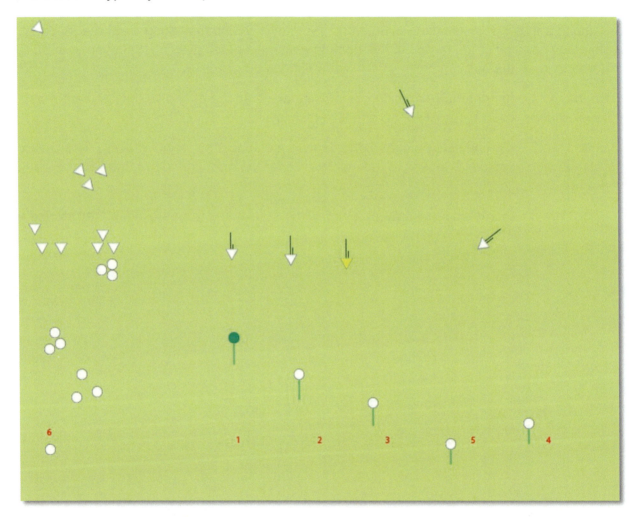

Notice that our target is the outside center, the slow defender. Although subtle, he and the D-IC are set so tight that the offensive OC *starts* with lane separation to the outside.

So, perhaps with this information, a "bounce" by the IC and OC would be in order to get past the tackle line before the D-SSW can get to his position. Let's take a look how it would diagram out:

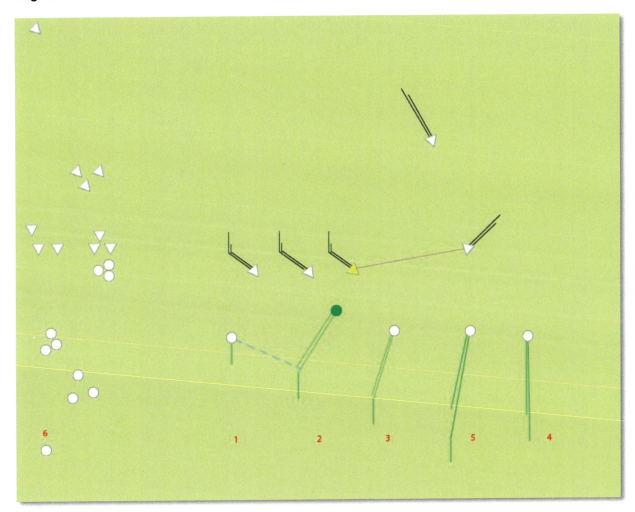

With a speed burst, the OC is testing the gap created between the D-OC and the D-SSW. The IC just needs to keep the pace up and provide a pass at the moment the OC is ready. Your OC, whom we have determined to be faster than the OC, has a better chance than not to hit this hole at full speed and break the tackle line. Does he score? It's certainly possible, with the D-FB forced to cover to the outside. The OC has created lane separation, and now simply needs to take advantage of it.

Preparation – *An Attack Key*

This method can be used endlessly, to create endless assumptions with which to operate during a match.

The method begins prior to a game, looking at video of the opposing team and searching for defects in the defense. A player or coach can watch for weaknesses during the game, and adjust strategy as the match goes on.

A team, as a practice, should then study video of their own team to understand which weaknesses were not exploited, and which opportunities were lost. Failing to review video of your own team's mistakes can create serious problems, whereby a team does not know why the fail, and why they succeed.

After a while, a team will develop a set of plays that exploit weaknesses on each part of the defensive backline, giving them a method to break the tackle line when each opportunity arises.

This key is a good example of what type of tactics may be helpful in each situation in which a full backline is available to attack:

Weakness	Play
Over aggressive D-IC	Dummy Scissor (FH & IC)
Over aggressive D-OC	Dummy Scissor (IC & OC)
Late D-IC	Crash (FH & IC)
Late or Early-Sliding/Pushing D-OC	Crash (FH & OC)
Non-switching defender	Scissor to that defender's original lane
Wide FH & IC	Crash / Dummy Scissor (FH & IC)
Wide IC & OC	Crash / Dummy Scissor (FH or IC w/ OC)
Wide SSW that does not fill	Crash (FH or OC w/ FB)
SSW that does fill	Pin to outside

Obviously, each tactic can be applied to other situations as well. Set pieces bring with them predictable, and thus favorable opportunities to apply tactics. Have a side of the scrum with a three on two advantage? Why not take it? By applying the tactics in this book to each scenario, you can be assured that you are pressuring the right part of the defense at the right time, and with the right tools.

Once a comprehensive kicking philosophy is applied to a rugby ground game, a team can then have a dual-threat attack plan. A team that is not seeing success in the ground game, but is still applying significant pressure on the ground, can leverage that pressure to improve their kicking game, and vice-versa. Well-placed tactical kicking only makes a ground game *more* formidable, as the defense attempts to cover all of the attacking methods applied by the offense.

Adjusting with Flat Backlines – *Complex Option Play*

An evolution of the above method has been to run an offensive backline relatively flat to the defense, using total rugby principles, and running up hard and repeatedly on a scissor and/or crash, but retaining several more options to get the ball to other players who are made available to the attack, such as forwards and spare backs.

A typical enhanced option play would have not only a scissor-crash set up, but a second crash option to the FB and a WSW moving outward (and behind the FH) to attack to the outside, as well as a flanker ready to receive a pass to the inside. This concept follows the same exact ideas and, if executed properly, may produce the same results. The FH becomes the command player that can make a decision on which option to select, and how to apply it.

These additional options are also a necessity – pressure hits a flat line much faster than a steep line, relatively speaking. So, the ball carrier must have several additional options to choose from based on an instant read of the field, conducted mid-play.

A multitude of such plays are possible. To catalogue each, possible combination of players and movements is outside of the scope of this book, and unnecessary. Those plays have been charted online and within clubs, with results ranging from the mundane to the bizarre. That's totally acceptable, and where the creativity should rest – with the individual clubs that hope to innovate in backline play calling.

It just takes imagination to tweak each and every one of these concepts, add attackers, and make new plays that have a positive impact for the offense. A quick Internet search of international highlights proves that experimentation can produce some incredible results.

The point is, regardless of how those plays are made, or how the backline is set to the line, or what type of movements are designed into the attack, those players must have options in the form of players that focus on breaking the tackle line first, and do so using initiative, speed, change of direction, off the ball movement, and communication.

Conclusion

With attention to detail and discipline, you can break the tackle line as a player or coach.

Since rugby is a thinking player's game, that must include learning about the why and the how of executing the most exciting maneuvers of the game. The ideas included here should give you a fresh edge, or a new understanding, for use on the pitch.

When the tactics start bearing fruit, you should see a few things change on the team that has applied them. The first sign is that your team will start making breaks of ten to twenty meters, and maybe more. Others should follow in quantity. You should see better attacks in the loose and in set plays. And the team may in fact begin to trust the backline. A functioning backline can improve the morale of the team in ways a functional pack cannot.

A problem will arise – what to do on breakaways? That's a good problem to have, on that can be resolved with further study, player support, and fitness. Have your support apply the tactics once they're there.

If the tactics produce a stalemate with your opponent, worry not. The tactics still place pressure on the weakest parts of a defense, and promise to "break the dam" late in that match or a match later in the season. A team that continually applies good tactics will be able to eventually capitalize on the benefits of deploying them.

So get out there, arm yourself with knowledge, and break the line!

Made in the USA
Las Vegas, NV
05 May 2021